TEN THOUSAND VENTURES

TEN THOUSAND VENTURES

poems by
Nevin Allen

First Print Edition / 001

Book cover and design by Spencer Stephens.

ISBN: 979-8-218-42262-2 (Paperback)

Library of Congress Control Number: 2024911559

Published by Nevin Allen, 2024

To anyone who's ever wondered if I'm writing about you:
I am.

I Oil

II Ink

III Blood

Ⅵ Honey

Ⅴ Water

"Our plans miscarry because they have no aim. When one knows not what harbor they make for, no wind is right."—Seneca

I

OIL

Who did you expect to save?

The tighter you hold a wounded animal

The closer its teeth to your throat

Declaration

to those who rage and those who gnash
who sell their tongues for fame and cash

to those who glower, terror-strung
entranced by pleasure's iron lung

the coming dread is heaven-sent
a flare of righteous discontent

for spineless dregs who hide behind
what warps the soul and traps the mind

ten thousand ventures still to learn
what you have built, my art will burn

Beacon

who are you to stay asleep?
wake up and smell the kingdom's fall
ash to ash and dust to dust—
even as man denies its fate.
the pact to never speak truth of the past

will fade as ancient spiders creep
and time buries us all.
letters carved in rotting rust
from a long-forgotten date
reveal the lies of our younger selves at last.

who are you to stay asleep?
though you may feel too weak to fight,
armor is forged and swords wrought
and banners heaved into the sky.
the herald overtakes the din.

the ore you mine is not too deep
to be touched by dawning light
forsake the lies you have been taught;
a crack, though many hands may pry
cannot outgrow the thing it's in.

who are you to stay asleep?
as the trumpet's blare grows louder still
and echoes through the valleys
recounting a battle still to come—
a timeless, desperate call to war

to pierce the endless folding heap
and shudder plants on windowsills.
to put wind in the sails of galleys
and give the hummingbirds their hum.
we gather here to ask once more

who are you to stay asleep?

.

Gravity's Favorites

Do the other heaven's angels vote supporting this divide?
If my silence is your weapon then my thunder is your test
If greener grass could grow unwatered surely someone lied
The storm comes irreversibly regardless of request

The other side is hateful but inspect your own four walls
The hinges plastered over to conceal the swinging joint
Your answer won't be found in purple prose or shopping malls
But from the mouth opposing your revolver's hollow point

You say faith is not worth dying for but sell your soul for oil
We can't make peace at home so we spill blood on foreign land
If we turn our gazes skyward will our hearts still curse the soil?
Could we outlive oblivion by standing hand in hand?

If only death can bring perfection, every saint is crowned in elegy
If only strength can bring connection, all birdsong is soliloquy

Inquisitor's Mirror

You wouldn't surrender decades
Just to make the sidewalks shine

If they were mine, you know that I would

I will find the narrow trail
No matter where I'm scattered
If I can't survive as a fountain
I'll outlive you as a footpath

You wouldn't embrace the burning
Just to share their flame yourself

If they were mine, you know that I would

Death is the penalty
For the unchanging heart
And endurance, like wisdom
Is rewarded with itself

You wouldn't sunder our kingdom
To erect four barren walls

      If they were mine, you know that I would

      I am not the pebble, friend
      Nor the sling that throws it
      I am its brief, great shadow
      As it shatters against your head

You wouldn't contrive a killing
To preserve mere pencil marks

      If they were mine, you know that I would

      I will strike your heel
      And if you crush my head
      My grin will remain my venom,
      Bright and final.

Testimony

The statue / welcomed the people
From the forehead to the / foundation

They were breaking / a boy standing next to me
I never saw him with a weapon

A witness may / be accepted / in a leadership role
Confront the war makers / shouting outside

> *Call your next / spy*
> *Call your next / snake*
> *Call your next / struggle*

Blame / dispersed / the flags

Tonight we're going to hold / the flares and the fires
We're going to build a barricade / from the far ends of the country
The first step toward the revolution

We should meet violence with / chanting and screaming
See you in the streets tonight

Liberation

your kingdom fading quickly
you survey the damage, sick
the fog, your toxic ignorance
grows dangerously thick
how many stabs must bear the word
to make the blood-stamp stick
your castle's wall is crumbling
with a hand on every brick

and now as times are getting hard
your plight is one most dire
in retrospect recanting
the great hubris of a liar
you trade their clean catharsis
for your fleeting, fake desire
I'm coming for your crown
so I can cast it in the fire

the battle lingers, heavy
but my spirit carries me
your dogs retreat, my swirling sword
tears through the tapestry
though you beg and you repent
nobody hears your plea
you made the people less than people
so the people made them free

Hymn for Rebuilding

o vengeful spirit
what holds you here
your body banished
no more to fear
the enemies
that once abounded
gone since the clarion
has three times sounded

o vagrant hunter
what guides your hand
to slay the creatures
that plague this land
your bow is drawn
your aim is steady
come high water or hell
you will be ready

o faithful watcher
what draws your eye
the sun is dawning
on crimson sky
lay bare the past
make plain the mystery
our time is only now
all else is history

o band of brothers
what sets us free
our fruitful venture
claims liberty
the king is dead
the flags are changing
our world as evermore
is rearranging

II

INK

Isn't it the strangest thing?

We are everything for a short while

And then we are nothing forever

Further Agency

I'll play again, but before the first move know
I'm tired of playing. every person a frozen piece:

the lies I told when I thought
I had hands enough to hold everyone close

and a handful somehow closer. stars in their own right—
slice them free, send them spinning.

consider the ceiling fan pantheon: the first team
orchestrating events for tomorrow's history books,

and the second soon to discover the universe
began on a sunday, a headline poised to make

nobody shift in their chair. if there were others,
we forgot them. December haze has us light-headed

and heavy-eyed, spending lifetimes trying to count
to one billion. goes quicker if you look away.

but you won't, and so I'm craving immortality—
 not the bloodbathed gothic sort, more cold-root:

the weed you can't quite yank. all metamorphic lust
self-defeats—the next thing will still want the next thing.

consider me now: I can take bad news standing up
but I'm no substitute for a warrior—I've found

nothing worth fighting for that survives a fight.
besides, we all lose, spend evenings in the forest

asking *who could have all this and still hunger?*
but we know. some things you admire by

forgetting them, a process that's more
complications than contact. in the meantime,

we're working on a way to have a plan
and yet no plan. goes quicker if you look away.

Negative Space

Before the blank space can be filled, the cursor blinks in waiting
A line that carries thirteen others' weight is still a loan
Before the voice can form midair, it waits in imitating
A raging calm acceptance knowing nothing can be known

Before the mind can know the shape, the fingers take to spinning
An execrated mirage in prostration to a map
Before the toxin hits the blood, the body takes to thinning
A poison poured through woven armor sticks in every gap

Before the doubts can reach the brain, they shiver up the spine
Denying thought to moonlight wishes rooted in neglect
Before the answer can be known, the questions step in line
Forgotten dusks have planned this rampant domino effect

Is your patience thinner than a sidewalk crack?
Is your shadow long enough to stab you in the back?

Exposition

why are we here?
those who ask already know
we gather in the name of gathering
to draw stones from destiny's bag

where the orange haze parts
the lavender blooms
amidst stolen, flaming tires
we grasp a chain into the sky

which reminds me of a building
I once saw crumble on the news
blissfully romancing gravity
becoming everything, falling down

so we're all on the same page
are we here seeking love or just
a defense against its opposite?
nobody can seem to agree

if we're still saving our lives
or finally spending them together.
our tongues don't need to match
if every name is just a reminder

of this gesture-torn separation
determined to complicate
our airborne rendezvous.
the truth is, with heavy heart

that despite all precautions
the time to outsmart death
was yesterday, darling
today there is only dancing.

so if you trip and fall through
to a sheet of blazing stars
look for me among them, wondering:
if there are people who are not poets,

how?

My Questions

It's me again– I've left my questions below.

Why does pretending feel like burning?
Why does remembering feel like burning?
Why does everything feel like burning?

What do you call the last shimmer before sunrise?

What does the inside of the mountain sound like?
Is the flag any lighter now that you've planted it in the dirt?
When do you expect it will flower?

What do you call the last shudder before sunrise?

Do love and doubt know who they are to one another?
Will the wind mourn me?
Can time feel us pushing back?

What do you call the last shiver before sunrise?

Will my father forgive me for wondering if he will forgive me?
Who watches me blink in the mirror?
Who wishes me luck when I waver?

What do you call the last shatter before sunrise?

Would it kill you to close your hand around mine?
Could you wither with any more care?
Could you die any quieter?

Have you ever stood on the edge of the world
Entranced and intrepid, ready to speak but not speaking?
If you haven't, well—I'll give you one guess what it feels like.

That's all. I hope to hear from you soon.

Fi Elvator (Stars Stir)

do we spend the correct amount of time looking up?
potholes are least ugly when they're most dangerous
(there is an elusive way to live happily in this place)

trimming bonsais, breeding poodles, fixing typos.
lightning does exactly the thing the name implies.
(there is food and drink and the topic is death)

I once knew a sun-burnt enchantress
who lost all faith in the concept of love.
(there is a secret second meaning of "cleave")

somewhere in the back corners of this cosmic estuary
a pair of clandestine agents live-drops a handful of stars.
(there is no way of knowing who is not watching)

deceivable, disputable, describable—all three mean killable.
the world was always effortlessly teeming with things
(there is an engineer responsible for their lack)

all our fears consider happening, then decide not to
we each spit out our greetings in a mad rush to get there
(there is rarely here)

two raindrops on a window pane compete for non-existence
and eight billion of us scream to be seen
(there is a way to survive this, but not unaltered)

Galaxy-Eyed Ramble

after some thought I've come to the realization
that I have two main options: write or die,
and while my loneliness has a preference
I plan to strike while the iron is hot
if only just to hope it stays hot forever

because the color red will never lie to you
considering it can't, and personally
I think that's sweet. like sledgehammers
and all other perfect things,
called upon for a singular purpose

and nothing else. the decision you made
to open the mailbox but not your hand
reminds me of a bird tattoo I once got
in the name of temporarily beautiful things,
but it flew away in the early days of last June.

since then i've been unable to decide
what I want, which makes everyone look
like a specially curated pop-up ad for
a problem I already have, but if I was looking
for casual insincerities I would save time
by learning to write down my own.

Memory of a Gentle Man

somewhere, a butterfly struggles to migrate
unaware it's flown into a nuclear reactor.
a boy's mouth closes adamantly on the wrong word
and says *I love you* by accident. he doesn't know yet
how expensive those words are—
I hope nobody ever dares to correct him.

do you think anyone told James when it started
that sometimes the end is just the end?
there were handshakes and well-wishes
maybe even some hugs, I suspect
but saying *I know* while comforting someone
is a shortcut to suddenly not knowing anything.

it's you and him and the silence at a table for two
which is to say it's you, watching what might be thunder
ripple through your espresso and vanish

I found him on the cobblestones, fists like
match-heads striking back at this shrinking world
waiting eagerly to be set aflame

I asked him how he braved it all each day
and he said, *because it will make a good story*
but who will tell that story? and he sighed
when I'm gone, I was hoping it'd be you

we had an understanding, him and I
that saying *I want to die* really means
when it's time for it all to be over, I need to be over too
and I need it all to be worth it

III

BLOOD

What's the point in getting up?

Each new ending's promise

Only reminds us of the old

Notes on Preservation

one day I'll fall asleep in a museum
with the record for most breaths held
while awaiting catastrophe.
(the plaque below will clarify
not one of them ever came.)

the curator at my exhibit drones,
here lies the boy who knows how to run
on ice, a feat for which there is no teacher.
before he knew how to fall, he fell
and he spent his life learning to stand.

if snow should teach us anything, it's this:
even angels fall asleep at the wrong times;
even demons go cold when they're threatened.
tomorrow, he'll wake up on somebody's couch,
heart attuned to another world.

he is the thief who outruns thieves
and the heart who changes hearts.
a voice that might be my mother whispers:
now you have felt the pain of twenty years
do you think you can bear twenty more?

oh, don't pretend like I'm so delicate.
I've been torn apart just by living
so what sting could death have left?
I've been force-fed more eternity
than my stomach can handle, friend.

I'm sick.

Visiting

break the chalk, pour the lemonade
by sundown our worries will have spent hours
unproductively thinking about us.

highways mimic forward movement
the way a heart recalls beating
fast for no reason except
possibility in the next hello.

only the wind remembers
what it means to move without caution
to rest lightly upon the earth
like a flare / like a finch / like a hurricane

garage door open, the selling's done
I ran out of reasons to keep
all the good things to myself.

the new coins flip like the old,
glint in a sunset bath that laughs
when a fire hydrant calls itself red.
I have a baseball but I've lost my glove

so we'll change the rules again
and my mom says be home by nine
or we'll disappear into the night
like a car / like a cloud / like a memory

Lux Nova

you'd never get close to an open flame, would you?
unless it was lit atop a sage-green column

in your grandmother's sink, warming
the eighth-to-last night of the year

honor-bound by some old gothic magic
or by her decades-long promise to you
(the latter is much more powerful)

it brings forth fortune in a radius denoted
by a sparrow in limerence with a jealous crow
two songs compete on a crackling wire

as it flies it circles the neighbor's backyard
and I know somehow that they're wrong
for burying an inverted statue

in the dirt of their family's well-loved land
but I look on, wondering in the dusk-damp
why we don't stain church windows anymore

I suppose all the colored light is waiting
to strike a pyre for burning paper or bones

and you told me yours were so cold that night, but
you'd never get close to an open flame, would you?

Keeping House

Atop a modest fortress flies a flag adorned pristine
The theory of the symbol warding tail and claw and tooth
The incremental solvents fail to scrub the garment clean
With sentimental residue it circumvents the truth

We all accept the iron glove but still deny the hand
The ivy thrives in ruin to entrap the castle's keep
Beneath a hail of sailing stones what righteous man would stand?
Simplicity through obligation's grip is never cheap

Treacherously step where future fruit will come to fall
Find hope in gazing forward to when none of this remains
What once decanted sunlight is now copper most banal
A distant din dissociates the agent from his stains

Will your boots not mark each other as they rush to claim renown?
Who baptizes a serpent out of fear that it will drown?

Broken Circle

what I miss most about childhood
is that a bond could be anything

a hand full of cashews silently exchanged
a hand reaching the top shelf for another
a hand to trace with my own

ties   /   ties   /   ties

what I miss most about adulthood
is that a bond could be anywhere

a word put to music in an empty car
a word through a phone before another goodbye
a word as a hot mug changes hands

ties   /   ties   /   ties

what I miss most about living
is that a bond could be anyone

a stranger you met in a grocery store line
a stranger you parted ways with long ago
a stranger you held until they were home

ties   /   ties   /   ties

what I miss most about dying
is that a bond could be anytime

a fourth-born refused admission, burned
a door swung shut down a darkened hall
a footstep ensnared, straining to break all the

ties   /   ties   /   ties

How to _____ a Fire

I. Light

if you were to know the exact moment of your death
would you be surprised to find it's already happened?
you died four seconds before eternity started
on a flat circle not unlike the one you now call upon
when you feel it running out of itself.
like a snake trying to choke on its own tail
without alerting his mother
who told him his eyes were too big for his stomach,
but also that there's room for dessert.
because what's the point in living
on a cliff if you don't jump
off it now and then? screaming
up until the instant before your head breaks
against the surface of the water and you gasp
the last ungrateful breath of a wide-eyed new soul,
born blazing

II. Love

did anyone tell you what came next?
that you'd raise a shifting voice, a crooked smile
he who wrestles / he who waits
who sits like a threat / stands like a promise
who comes out stung and swinging
scared / scarred / sacred boy

but then, which one do you see?
is he a brutal man with a gentle side?
is the opposite even possible?
I admire your abandon, but I pray
you'll abandon even him one day.
he is not here / (he is not held)

when the thing we thought was life
became a part of itself, we turned to
the forgivers / the returners / the redeemers
because speaking will wound the silence
but waiting is surrendering. consider
your busy heart, its teeming lobby.
when it dies, is it opening or closing?

III. Lose

you hold a man who was somehow born
containing a complete list of all the things
that can be raised. this includes:
armies, suspicions, walls, barns, and hell
not one of which can bring him down,
and never for lack of trying.

I wonder most what you thought of him
when he first sparked through, oblivious.
those sun-scoured moments of silence
described in another way:
the sands and seeds, the searching.
the sudden silence of the prophet

he is a diligent space-searcher
who hums against hollows,
dreaming of more elegant ways
to dispose of everything.
the black hole is his favorite,
but this he does not know:
when it dies, is it opening or closing?

IV. Leave

I miss when I could lie to people
and still be right about them every time
but even now I've found few paradoxes
not worth chewing on.
lately, this question:
who were you to me before I knew who you were?
turns out,

      You were a grassroots print campaign against paper waste.

      You were the headline-barking spokesman
      for cutting-edge new ways to remain inaudible.

      You were a teacher for remedial courses
      on how to take the pressure off the wound
      before it was a wound.

      You were the patron saint of losing faith in it all
      and unbelieved even yourself back out of existence.

      You were the fear that I'd misunderstand who you were.

Meanwhile, I've been wandering
I've been wavering
I've been whispering

How much have we lost in this tear / in this time / in this tension?
How much could we still find?

Museum

were the stars brighter then?
staring faces always pressed
into reverent, wondrous scrutiny

as if they didn't know yet
how to scream in a way
the future could clearly hear

smothered by a sculpted mask
that were it one shade more alive
would have shattered

and left us nothing at all
to find our half-myths in

or are we consanguineous with their gods?
did we trade our eternity of sunlight
for a single flickering candle
and the smell of each other's skin?

VI

HONEY

Is there ever enough time?

I will never forgive you fully

And I will never hang up first

Setup

Taken back, a film reel spent, a broken memory burned
A darkened room ensconced in waiting strangers I'll twice meet
Prismatic potions mixed onto a labile canvas turned
Emblazoned on my heart with black machinery and heat

Two eyes I drank in fortnights past stared back at me that night
As indistinct yet haunting as the patterns in my sleep
A crack had formed in sharpened ocean wary of your slight
Sensations piled high atop an indistinct red heap

I tasted with a foreign tongue a nectar from afar
A ship marooned off darkened shore in all-consuming ice
It tuned to life a memory retained, somehow ajar
Both alike in dignity, both die at whim of dice

The look you gave me left a wound I fear will never heal
But there exists no camera yet to capture how I feel

New Wine

it is endless night
and there is a strange piece of her upstairs

labeled hypnotic colors beyond my reach
left basking in a reflection off of infinite walls
I am sipping cranberry juice like the hours of the dark

sweet and gentle and tart and violent but old,
grown in flooded swamps filled with crawling things
that drag nails across unfinished wood,
a scraping sound so loud I can't quite hear it
I can only bathe and grit my molars and wonder.

it would be the easiest thing in the world
to never hunger or thirst or need again

to wade into the mire that precludes the after-death
where heads are checked at the door
and hearts left out for taste-testing

eyes closed in pulsing void, dancing to whatever rhythm.
it would be easy to lose my shoes in that room
but my eyes are open and I am parched and I need to scream
and she is upstairs,
sleeping.

I Hesitate to

imagine the wide-mouthed idiocy of the fig
as it apologizes to the trapped wasp
thinking well, you were (are) beautiful
but now that I have you, you're dissolving
and try as we might it seems you are stuck
to me.

turn out the second story ceiling lights
so the neighbors won't speculate
if I'm the sort of lover who can pretend
to see you, or just the kind who chooses
to believe that you mean what you say
to me.

I wanted to close the window and scream
what, this star-slain seeker?
his saint-stained edifice was found
dead but still dying, thrashing his skull
and swollen eyes every which way except
to me.

it pained me to hear that you
still remembered the version of me
who wouldn't need to breathe deeply
before answering each of your questions
and worse, you actually preferred him
to me.

Companion

living forever is no protection
from falling forever.
peering outwards, reaching up
towards this woman I know like
 a sniper knows a brain scan
he hasn't seen yet. *it will work,*
this sudden transformation. it has to.

look at her.
jackhammered gemstone, waning iris
sacred vessel of the moon.
magnetic tidal artifact,
churning electric sheen.
what promise, what power.

but me.
I'm not the man I was four days ago,
I'm just the boy I was last year.

my soul has firewalls older than my soul.

if I shed my armor my skin will follow,
an old t-shirt snagging on a hoodie.
she appraises what's beneath:
what polished teeth you have
what perfect, ancient bones

I'm late to my own surprise party.
I'll find her in the wreckage
or I'll leave her in the past.

A _____ Shadow

I. Wandering

your thoughts cannot trouble you
if you dump them all out
onto paper or canvas

rain cleaving snow
in a pointillist matrix
with just enough space
between the pen and the page

to put everything you're thinking
into a box no heavier than your brain
but fifty times bigger, and silver

so congratulations!
you tricked them into admitting
to exactly what you were afraid of

after all, this is the third time
you've tried to make a thing
deserving of the vilest name
only to look up and realize
you don't know what it's called

II. Great

it is her lips that devastate.
there is a wan, shallow beauty
in hearing the struggle

that drenched you, nameless
for two months or as many years
summarized in a sentence
from the mouth of a stranger

and you can't even get it
tattooed on your tombstone
because that would be plagiarism

which to the immortal, the ink-soul
is a lower blow than murder
so you sit and rearrange the words

writing not so much stories
as conversations you wish you had
with another person, which is to say
a hand that's not strictly yours
but doesn't mind being in your hair

Flashbulb

see here, an unstoppable child
fingers splayed, determined to explode the camera.
she knows the truth in an uncomplicated way:
we are doing the world wrong.
it is (we are) temporary
no amount of wait-no-stop-ing
can make it less so.
it is fleeting, and we must listen to the rain.

twenty years later, her hand's closed
around something—you can't see what
as the far child falls, knee-broke
in worship to your deity, a perfected frontal lobe,
stamped—gushing and almost red.
she's a full picture now—tongues and teeth
and an impossible appetite for what she's caught
but she's saving it for later

Web Disambiguation

so here we are again, as always
finding ourselves on the precipice
of some undocumentable occurrence

I have a vial of your poison on my shelf
which I sip on occasion to remind me that yes,
forgetting you will still kill me.

a seven-hundred mile glance
off my armor which I wear overtop
a mounting pile of questions but

if yours is beneath your skin
I suppose we're both stuck here wishing
the other one would reach for the dial.

until one of us does we are, as ever
two strangers in sunglasses
left wondering if the other is staring

beneath seagulls that couldn't care less
about our lustful quarrel, our half-war
because to them we are one second closer

to being lifeless corpses, eroding rock
meaningless obscenities carelessly cast
into the seafoam even they soar above

V

WATER

Have you considered it?

How perfect we all could be

If we just stopped being afraid?

How to Time - Bathe

if you want to see the picture fully
you must wash it from your wrist
because it will not wait, won't inhale
won't let you slip away

        it will only glisten around you
        an un-made non-thing in the half-light
        that swirls in the all and the everything
        adamantine, clandestine thoroughfare

so momentarily become a large reptile
or a photo of a bygone winter
moving slower the more you're watched
like the second hand circling back around

        and when autumn finally breaks
        we'll all be Paul lying on the rug again
        the thunder resting upon us
        like heaven's weighted blanket

if you feel old hatred everywhere
create a new nowhere and stay
rest your throat for the night
and let your eyes do the screaming

        it's days like these we learn to hold
        the future like a wounded owl
        we must teach each other
        where to keep it / what to call it / when to let it go

though it may seem now that existing
means re-learning language every day
we are shards of a twice-shattered earth, you and I
we are fragments of the same dream

The New Momentum

I often wonder if my tepid, bloodless-seeming brain
Can read the words without that cursed black italic tilt
Pursued like fish through cities under one eternal crane
A magnetic illusion seeking blade but finding hilt

The itch that Earth is infinite is hollow still to prove
Though frozen water cannot ripple hopeful to forgive
A marble is not stagnant though it lashes to its groove
We live to chase the truth, but we forget to truly live

The wandering hands probe landscapes married to the whitest noise
A map of places righteous roaming hummingbirds can rest
If even for a moment weightless wings should shed their poise
From flowers falls the sun into a field of finite jest

But we, the gorgeous strangers, can proclaim that we were there
When the eyes inside the mirror found an answer to despair

Spending Summer

getting to know myself has proven to be painting
the corners of a cornerless space.
when the music stops, I'm standing with a brush just—

      walking home from work and I'm in a cavern
      watching a swirling ceiling become a sky
      there are dots in the dark that might be stars
      or falling glass, blown sea-sparks in the setting sun

      same as the bottles that litter the road
      once perfected in their ability to hold nothing
      but the light as it falls, pulled to earth by a whisper
      and un-broken by a curse, but I don't—

            remember not wanting, just like I don't know how it felt
            to be unborn, flush with promise and patience
            uncontaminated by the knowledge that one day I will gasp
            not for air, but for sharing another's

            nose nestled in the space between the ears and lips
            where I find speckled, asymmetrical constellations
            that perhaps her lovers have named
            but only she has truly known—

waiting.

The Clematis _____

I. Wants

the thing about loving artists
is you never need to remind them
of how temporary it all is

but now I've traded the camera
of yet another glowing redhead
for time, which just feels like recoil
slamming me back and forth

for as many shots as it takes
to immobilize the gorgeous force
that hounded me, sesquipedalian
for the better part of a year
(or more than half of it anyway)

I'm told somewhere far north is burning
but something else is in the air

II. Wilts

I've been redesigning my body
into a freshly antithetical entity
that can allegedly withstand
a direct glance from itself

but since I'm always the last to know
tell me this: is there a place you'd rather be
than rattling around inside my brain?

my new eyes can't tell if you're dancing
or treading water, and though my tongue
is trapped behind the same ordinary grin
as before, I can't deter it
from spilling the most random truth:

I am surrounded by beautiful things
I am tragically unprepared to want

III. Waits

I've never told the whole truth
to people I expect to see again
it leaves my lips with nothing to be
except the shield against bored teeth gnashing
flirtatiously at the pin of a grenade

I've got no choice but to slyly remark
you know these things were made
to obliterate buildings full of enemies?

but between us is just a coffee table
because we thought it would gather friends
(nevermind lovers, they'll settle anywhere)

though the chemistry may be delayed
I will linger until the dust starts to clear,
a sigh amongst the smithereens.

IV. Wins

I'm always wary of gentle people
with long hair because it means
they've found a stranger form of revenge.

I once shook a man's hand
and as I met his gaze got the sense
I was the first to survive doing so.

I wondered then and still now
how many worlds he ended before
realizing his, too, would end one day
and be consumed by its vestiges

like a long-forgotten nuclear reactor,
cherished again in time
for the same reason it was despised:
it's a picture of a love we cannot own.

Source Code

healing has always just been learning
I am a this-makes-that sort of person
like bullets make inconvenient leaks in things
and April makes fools of us all

Sunday

The perfect day was one on which the sun did never rise
A steaming beverage fast imbibed in blushing histamine
The rain descending flatly from the melting, teary skies
Became an ornamental swatch as you surveyed the scene
Till hell recalls its extant hound
Rebuke the sky, rebuke the ground

On grayest evenings breathe the sweetest perfume, that is air
Its scent remembered in a room that looks like all the rest
Eyes never meet nor fingers touch but both are done with care
A silver bird constructing without haste a flowered nest
While beauty blossoms all around
Rebuke the sky, forgive the ground

She sighs in seeking rest or imitating some refrain
A peace in silence thundering with every rising breath
She thinks of nothing lost tonight nor anything to gain
Delightfully resplendent proof of concept for her death
Before your heart can make a sound
Forgive the sky, forgive the ground

Dedication

to those who love and those who long
who stay up late ensconced in song

to those who wander, midnight-dazed
the sunrise-gauzed who step unfazed

to lend their unrelenting voice
in harmony, lamenting choice

should freedom be the greatest curse
til dying we complete this verse

ten thousand ventures coalesce
what time has baned, my art will bless

"As each day arises, welcome it as the very best day of all, and make it your own possession. We must seize what flees."—Seneca

Notes

"Testimony" is written only using words and phrases recorded from the prosecution witnesses in the trial of the so-called "Conspiracy Eight." The slashes indicate where phrases were cut or spliced.

"Fi Evator (Stars Stir)" takes both its title and its last line from damaged or misquoted signage. Fi Evator comes from a damaged "ELEVATOR," while Stars and Stir are both corruptions of "STAIRS."

"Web Disambiguation" is tragically not a real Wikipedia article.

Thank you to the editors of the publications where these poems have previously appeared: "Sunday" in *Vocivia*, "I Hesitate To" and "A _____ Shadow" in *Perfumed Pages*, and "My Questions" in *Gypsophila*. Your encouragement saw this book through to the finish line.

Acknowledgements

I never could have written *Ten Thousand Ventures* alone. I would like to thank:

All the people I subjected to unfinished versions of my work, for their critique and their patience. You, my friends, are the ones that keep me writing.

My editors **Riley Heath** and **Courtney Kehler,** for forcing me to make sense.

Mom & Dad, for supporting even what you couldn't understand, and easing even what you couldn't prevent.

Lily, for believing me. For believing in me.

Ollie, for being right the entire time.

Spencer. For the cover, for the companionship, and for reminding me what the whole thing was about. May the future you dream of one day come to pass.

Mrs. Robinson, for telling me to never stop writing poetry. I never will.

The Author

Nevin Allen is a Pennsylvania-born screenwriter and poet currently studying Dramatic Writing at the Savannah College of Art and Design. He spends his free time admiring imposing artworks, reading strange books, and learning fun facts about birds. *Ten Thousand Ventures* is Nevin's first book.